STOP JUDGING ME

JENISH SAHER

XpressPublishing
An imprint of Notion Press

XpressPublishing
An imprint of Notion Press

No.8, 3rd Cross Street,CIT Colony,
Mylapore, Chennai, Tamil Nadu-600004

ISBN 978-1-64951-436-3

STOP JUDGING ME

JENISH SAHER

Contents

Foreword

We are practically judged by almost everyone, in all domains of our life. Let's find a permanent solution on how to deal with people who judge you negatively. This book will give you answers to your questions related to being judgmental and how it will identify you as a person based on your behaviour.

Preface

I wrote this book because there was and is still a time where I am particularly judged unjustly. It hurt me a lot. I went through a lot of psychological problems in my life. But, luckily as I am a psychology student I found solutions to my problems and learnt how to deal with it.

Acknowledgements

In the 21st Century, It's almost impossible to not judge anyone. We have developed the habit of passing a comment or expressing your opinion about others within seconds. A corporate image consultant and personal brand strategist called Anna Hinson said "within the first 7 seconds of meeting someone, our mind makes 11 different decisions about them including their intelligence, socioeconomic status, education, competence and trustworthiness". Well, our human mind is like a central processing unit, which processes millions of thoughts which run across our mind, be it positive or negative, which then reflects our exterior behavior. We definitely cannot stop our thoughts. But, we can definitely change the way we judge others. We need to be very particular while commenting on others. Let's embrace the truth and learn the facts of how to deal with judgments across all domains of our life. I completely disagree with those people who judge negatively, indirectly hurt, and impose their beliefs onto you. It's ethically not right. And certainly not correct when some people just gather and gossip about you all the time. And it's extremely annoying when you are aware of that fact. Of course, these people volunteer to gossip. You will find these specific gangs everywhere be it in your colony, friend circles, church groups, colleagues at work, family members, their targets are to remove all the inabilities about you and suggesting you to follow their own beliefs. I have noticed that people enjoy gossip not realizing that they are forming a bad habit. Gossiping, expressing your opinion, or passing wrong comments are all related to judging others. Sometimes we all are perceived wrong. And it hurts deeply. Especially when you know that you have done nothing wrong. Of course, nobody is perfect, we are humans and we do make mistakes. But everybody at some point in life, you will come across a person who will backstab, gossip, hurt, put you down, pass unjust comments on you. It's high time we learn to bring out a solution to this problem rather than complaining about it all the time.

CHAPTER ONE

RIGHT TO CHOOSE

"Let us choose what is right; let us know among ourselves what is good" (Job 34:4). Every individual has a right to choose what they want. Life is full of choices that you make. It all depends on you at the end. Every single day we struggle to make choices of our own. Some choices are so hard to make while, some just come along your way very easily. Nobody's life is so simple. You may be the richest man in the city, but you have got to make decisions. None of us can escape making decisions. You ought to choose between the two or more options kept in front of you. You cannot sail in both the boats putting one leg in each of them, you will drown for sure. Some decisions give you great success and some lead to failure. Neal Boortz correctly said in one of his quotes, "The key to accepting responsibility for your life is to accept the fact that your choices, every one of them, are leading you inexorably to either success or failure, however you define those terms".

Every decision you make has its own consequences attached to it. You have got to be more careful while picking the right one. As one of the quotes says, "The more decisions that you are forced to make alone, the more you are aware of your freedom to choose". by Thornton wilder.

The hard decisions are very heartbreaking and stressful but sometimes it leaves you with no other option but only one. That one option is your only way out, whether you like it or not. When we lose someone who was really close to you, could be mom, dad, siblings, best friend in such case you are left with no option but to let go. We know they cannot come back to life. It's so devastating and stressful at the same time. We are helpless here and leave us with the only option to accept reality. Well, one could be in extreme pain, grief but someday you need to let go and move on. It's sad but the truth. "Decisions are the hardest thing to make especially when it is a choice between where you should be and where you want to be" - Anonymous.

For instance, you notice students after appearing for the 10th & 12th board examinations are confused with regard to selecting which subject to specialize in. Because that one decision for selecting a particular specialization could change their entire life. Students are referred to career counselors so that they are not confused and guided well for the upcoming future. At the same time, there are students who do exactly what their parents want them to do. If they suggest becoming a doctor for instance, so be it. The child is simply gulping in the poison, just to make his parents happy, suppressing his own choice. Well, he might keep up to his parent's decisions. But gradually will fall apart. The question is what's wrong? Are you happy with what you're doing ? Are you making a decision for yourself or let others make them for you?

We all have our regrets, at least once in lifetime. But, that is how life works. Isn't it ? We cannot have everything at all times and neither are you like a superman who would know which direction you should take. There is no one who will never regret in his lifetime. We can't do anything here. Because there is no mastery in decision making. One thing we can do is to become better at it. By better, I mean you will improve by making decisions someday and it comes with maturity and understanding and sometimes with acceptance. According to the Holy Bible, the scripture says, And the Lord commanded the man, saying, "you may surely eat of every tree of the garden, but of the tree of the knowledge of good and evil you shall not eat, for in the day that you eat of it you shall surely die"(Genesis 2:16-17). The decision was clearly presented to Adam, to eat from all the trees in the garden only. Later, God saw that Adam was lonely, so he created a woman for him so that she could accompany him and not feel lonely all the time. "So the lord God caused a deep sleep to fall upon the man, and while he slept took one of his ribs and closed up it's place with flesh and the rib that the lord God had taken from the man he made into a woman and brought her to the man"(Genesis 2: 21,22). The woman was named Eve. When God had instructed them to not eat of the tree of knowledge, he meant something more divine which Adam and Eve didn't take seriously. God just wanted both of them to simply trust as well as obey him. As you continue to read the scriptures you will get to know that Eve sinned and ate from the very same tree which the lord particularly told her to avoid eating from. The serpent tricked Eve and she ate of the tree. By portraying the example of Adam and Eve was to determine that, both of them had a decision to make. They had to think why god specifically denied having from that tree which was in the middle of the garden. We all know, god is wise enough to tell us anything. The only reason why he didn't convey to Adam of what could be the consequences after eating from the tree of knowledge is because he wanted to see how much the first man on earth that he created trusted and obeyed him or not. Similarly, just as Adam and Eve had to make the right choice or judge wisely, we too need to be very peculiar in our choices, decisions we make on a daily basis and the judgment you make for others.

If you are weak at making decisions, it's fine. But, decisions are to be made anyhow. Everyday choices teach you that the prior decisions you took were beneficial or not, are they giving you progress or are you facing the consequences of that one decision which you took earlier. Nothing to worry. Either way you are learning something.

CHAPTER TWO

LEAVE ME ALONE

An American women's magazine called, Allure focused on beauty conducted a national survey in the hopes of finding out just how much we judge ourselves and others, both in the real world and on social media. This article was written by Danielle pergament on February 10, 2016. She stated, "we judge, even if we try not to. On one hand, being judgmental is part of being human. On the other hand, have we made it into an art form. 80% of people said everyone judges other people's looks. But the good news is that even more of us around 84% are trying to be less judgmental". We continuously keep judging people by their looks, not knowing how they are actually by heart. For instance, when I used to study in Mumbai, India. During my college day, I used to go every day for an evening walk at Bandra - Worli sea face. I used to notice a lot of women wearing sports shoes with salwar. Well, for me it doesn't matter much. But one of my friends always laughs and judges the women's attire. She makes weird faces and goes blank with a question mark on her face, and says, "can't they simply put on a top and a track pant"! to which I replied, "well maybe they don't have time to change their clothes, so they come with whatever they are wearing the whole day long". There is this beautiful verse, which I came through while reading my Bible.

"For you were called to freedom, brothers. Only do not use your freedom as an opportunity for the flesh, but through love serve one another. For the whole law is fulfilled in one word. You shall love your neighbor as yourself"(Galatians 5:13-14).

Just imagine, if someone judges you on the basis of your looks, caste, language, and simply everything you do on a daily basis. Wouldn't it be irritating? Or would you like to entertain all the comments, opinions of others regarding you all the time? I am sure someday you will say, "Oh come on shut up, just let me be". we cannot entirely stop ourselves from being judgmental, but to maintain the peace, love and freedom amongst ourselves we just need to leave them alone. We cannot always keep interfering into others' business. It's like pointing your finger towards others, not realizing the other three fingers are pointing back towards you.

Why do you think people will hide all the important talks of their family and not let them out for others to discuss or give opinions on them?

Have you ever thought about it? Well, it's simply because they are indirectly telling you to just leave them alone and let them be. They are pushing you out so that you don't continuously poke your dirty nose into other peoples life causing trouble to them. Try to learn something out of it. It's wise enough to try not to judge rather than being judgmental. If you do, you will end up with a lot of psychological problems like over thinking, anxiety, unnecessary stress, jealousy. Instead of being concerned about your own life, you will always end your days thinking about another person.

Spiritually speaking, we all fall short of God's grace every day. That is the only reason we pray and we are taught to pray by our parents. It's a kind of meditation that we all do, to pass by each day. As it is correctly pointed out in the book of (James 4:6). Yet the lord makes it sure to give each and every one of us to be filled with his grace. Therefore, "God opposes the proud but gives grace to the humble". One will try not to judge only and only when God gives his grace to you. Which means you have ought to leave them alone. By being judgmental you show you're not humble, henceforth God will not give you his grace, because it defines you as if you're proud enough and taking the law into your hands.

CHAPTER THREE

JUDGING CHOKES LOVE

"Owe no one anything, except to love each other, for the one who loves another has fulfilled the law"(Romans 13:8).

What keeps us from fulfilling the law of love which is easily exemplified by Jesus and laid out in the scriptures? We actually position ourselves as judges of others rather than simply as lovers of others said by Greg Boyd in one of his articles. Are we loving others? We tend to judge others so instinctively where we begin to assume that we are right by our motive to judge.

This is the only reason we end up overlooking the fact that our judgments are choking our love and are preventing us from living in the truth, which God first created us to follow and live to.

For instance, imagine you have just made a new friend in college both of you'll get along really well. Your friend is very funny, loving and talkative. You love to spend time together. Suddenly, one fine day your friend ignores you and is acting weird with you. Now, of course you don't find your friend loving and talkative because you're annoyed by the fact that she is ignoring you. Then, you see your friend in pain and is crying. Now, you feel compassionate towards your friend and sit to talk with her. You know she was acting weird because she was in pain and had some problems at home of which she was struggling a lot with. What do we learn from this example?

1. Examine yourself: sometimes, we may be judging someone for something that we do ourselves. For example, when you say, "this man knows nothing, ask yourself was there a time when I knew nothing" ? of course, yes we all have been through that stage where we knew nothing.

2. Just be happy and proud of yourself. Basically lifting up your self - esteem. If you are, for example, happy with the clothes you wear, you won't judge other people's clothing style. In short, be content with whatever is available to you at the moment.

3. Once Will Smith said, "because, in all honesty, everyone is struggling. Some people are better at hiding it than others". It's like walking into my shoes and you will understand what I am going through.

There are going to be people, where they will make things difficult for you and disagree with. But that shouldn't bother you so much because judging a person does not define who they are, it defines who you are. It's about their own insecurities, limitations and needs. Don't take in that unnecessary suffering too personally. It will make you clog your mind completely there will be no possibility to let positive thoughts enter your mind or love one another. As it is said by Mother Teresa. "If you judge people, you have no time to love them". We say to love is easy, well let's be honest. It's not as easy as it seems like. I am not referring to romance love here, but about the genuine love which comes out from the bottom of your heart for others. To respect, accept the people as they are. The all mighty lord exactly did the same , he accepted us just the way we are, didn't differentiate between the wise and the weak, never compared our inabilities. So my question to you is , why do we judge and differentiate amongst us? Andy Puddicombe, an author wrote in his article. "Not judging is a gift we can give to others". When we don't love someone, we either become their enemies or become jealous. Because by feeling jealous we simply cannot achieve what the opposite person has with them. Often judgments are associated with jealousy. If you say, I am not jealous of that particular person then why are you judging that person unjustly ? Practically speaking, you judge someone because either you like something about them or not. If you like something then it's fine because it's positive. But when u don't like something for example, you don't like the dress that a lady is wearing. Well in that case ,you do not get the opportunity to judge her likes and dislikes. Because it's actually up to her. She will wear anything she pleases. Three things you are absolutely wrong about, one if you are passing a comment on her dress then either you want the same dress as her which is imposing jealousy, two you are simply not liking her dressing sense or three you are bored, unhappy and not satisfied with your own life, so you like poking your nose into others business. Well as I said earlier, it's not your place to judge either way. The authority to judge is given to the most superior being of all. That is god. Isn't it why we say, Karma will show you back? The lord says, "Do not judge, and you will not be judged. Do not condemn and you will not be condemned. Forgive and you will be forgiven. Give and it will be given to you a good measure" (Luke 6:37,38). This is the only way to maintain your blessings.

CHAPTER FOUR

PERCEPTIONS

Perceptions vary from each other, isn't it? Well, practically it goes like this. Awesome! Said a friend of mine, who just heard a new track of rock music which was released a week ago. To which I replied, really? with sarcasm. She had a different opinion about the particular type of music, and she found it really amazing and awesome to hear; on the contrary, I didn't seem to agree with her. One out of ten people are definitely not gonna agree with your opinion. So what??? In the end, what happens is we make our perception a reality. We need to understand that your friend said Awesome! Because she saw through her own perceptual lens and she made the judgment.

"We can't tell the difference between what our opinion is and what the reality is". Rubin goddam a clinical psychologist wrote in one of his articles.

There is always a technique and a way to express yourself. The harsh language we use gives us the ultimate final result of our behavior.

It is said in Acceptance and commitment therapy, "we don't see things for what they are, we see things through the lens of our mind".

For example, an actress like Kangana Ranaut wins an Oscar award for Best Actress, 2020. Now whether you call her stupid, beautiful, ugly, dumb, well don't matter because ultimately won the best actress award. The question is how did she win? But obviously, there are people who loved her movies, as opposed to those who didn't like her movies.

Similarly, one of my college friends was judged like this, he must be her boyfriend.....why? I suppose because she walked in with a boy beside her, like really?? He could just be a friend or her brother. Why don't you see the things, the way they are and always impose your thought, mind to it. Always look on the bright side of life.

So the next time you judge someone or something be very selective and peculiar of your words, tone, behavior. Because your one perception, which according to you is right about a person or a thing may not be the same as others perceive the world. Judgments made by us are our way of perceiving the world. It's just one perspective. And you know you cannot make any judgments as facts. Because only when you try to make those judgments factual or start making it seem like real you end up messing with your mind.

Messing with your mind, I literally mean Assumptions. Making assumptions simply because you made it purposely look like it's real and think it's the truth.

For instance, you will come across this one person who will talk maliciously about someone who is not present at the point. so, when 'A' is talking to 'B' about 'C' what happens is it seems very surprising to me that 'B' is actually listening and believing whatever 'A' has to say about 'C'.

Now, my question is how can 'B' actually believe whatever 'A' is saying about 'C'? It could be that 'A' is purposely speaking all bad about 'C' to 'B' because 'A' is holding a grudge against 'C'. Well, in my opinion, I wouldn't believe whatever 'A' has to say about 'C' unless I get to see it with my own conscience. Because whatever 'A' has to say about 'C'. 'A' makes it sure enough that to make 'B' believe in her, Will starts making assumptions, making stories. I feel even if you choose one of your family members, you shouldn't believe whatever he/she speaks about unless you're completely aware of and know or have perceived it with your own eyes. To some up with a quote by Don Miguel Ruiz from his book, the four agreements, the message goes like this;

"We make the assumption that everyone sees life the way we do. We assume that others think the way we think, feel the way we feel, judge the way we judge, and abuse the way we abuse. This is the biggest assumption that humans make. And this is why we have a fear of being ourselves around others. Because we think everyone else will judge us, victimize us, abuse us, and blame us as we do ourselves. So even before others have a chance to reject us we have already rejected ourselves".

CHAPTER FIVE

SUBCONSCIOUS MIND

The subconscious mind is the most powerful one. when compared to the conscious and unconscious mind it stores all the knowledge, thoughts, feelings, experiences, habits, memories etc., This brain dominates over the conscious and unconscious mind also is your guidance system. Your subconscious mind is in control at least 95% of every day. It practically records everything we encounter.

Making negative judgments of all types will form a habit. Let's concentrate more towards negative habits. Every time when you find people who have something negative to say about another person, try to distance yourself from them. Because they have this dirty and the most filthy habit which will probably pull you in along with them. whenever they are free you will definitely find them passing comments, making wrong judgments, having no knowledge about that particular person. Preferably not knowing what hardships that person must have gone through. It's like they have nothing more important but to backbite all the wrong about someone or the other.

Good habits like respecting ourselves, brushing our teeth in the morning, having breakfast, following all the traffic rules. These habits you perform without having to think them over, and they become an automatic response. We perform based on our daily tasks. Henceforth, leading to good healthy habits.

Similarly, bad habits like backbiting about others whenever free, want to be like the center of attraction discussing somebody wrongly just to prove your point. There are an endless number of examples.

When you harbour that bad behavior every day, it forms a serious bad habit which you will continue to do every day. Because the subconscious mind is recording your day to day behavior and is storing it permanently. Now, when it has stored your feelings, thoughts for someone it will reflect back whatever you have stored in your subconscious mind for a very long time. So one of the verses from the bible says, "Do not be conformed to the pattern of the word but be transformed by the renewing of your mind, that by testing you may discern what is the will of God, what is good and acceptable and perfect"(Roman 12:2).

The consequences of harbouring bad habits:

1. Ultimately, you will somehow end up only talking bad and negative about anybody. Be it a strong person, yet you will judge him/her even if you don't have anything to do with that stranger who is just walking past you.

2. You will develop a lot of frustration because you're anyways feeding those negative thoughts and feelings continuously.

3.You will develop a sense of fear. From fear, it will develop a big amount of anxiety in you.

4. Probably you could even face insomnia because of stress and anxiety.

All these problems occur because you are happily harboring and very easily entertaining the negativity around you by talking unjustly about somebody. As a result, just take a look who is suffering the most? It's you and only you facing mental stress as well as physical issues. Where is the peace here? What's wrong?

Well, I would say practically everything is wrong about you.

Because the Lord says to maintain the peace that I have given you. That peace comes from prayers, a meditation on the word of God. As rightly pointed out in this specific verse of the bible.

"Peace I leave with you; my peace I give to you. Not as the world gives do I give to you. Let not your hearts be troubled, neither let them be afraid" (John 14:27).

Watch your mouth, before you hurt anyone. Words once said cannot be taken back. You cannot rewind backwards, like in the movies. Be very careful to even speak wrong about anyone, whether your back biting or directly speaking to someone. For you do not know what battle that particular person is fighting. Of course, we all go through hardships and struggle with almost everything. The only difference is, there are different levels of hardships or struggles. For example, your friend is facing a tremendous amount of trouble in her relationship. Somebody out there is struggling to make their ends meet every single day. Whereas you could be very well, stable enough with your financial status. For your reference, I came across this verse in the bible.

"It is not what goes into the mouth that defiles a person, but what comes out of the mouth; this defiles a person". Do you not see that whatever goes into the mouth passes into the stomach and is expelled?

But what comes out of the mouth proceeds from the heart, and this defiles a person.

"For out of the heart come evil thoughts murder, adultery, sexual immorality, theft, false witness, slander. These are what defile a person. But to eat with unwashed hands does not defile anyone"(Matthew 15:11,17-20).

Some so-called "Christians" are aware of this very well, yet they themselves choose to continuously hurt people unjustly. They are so enthusiastic to pull the trigger whenever they feel like. It is not only for Christians but to other people out there who are repeatedly showing unworthy behavior. Some are so stubborn and arrogant as if, it seems they are the only king and queen of this universe not realizing these people have come up from the very same trash that they now associate other people with.

In the early 20th century, a Gestalt psychologist Fritz Heider known as the father of attribution theory. He said that "People make attribution based on their own wants and needs which are, therefore, often skewed". He further went on to explain this tendency was rooted in a need to maintain a positive self-concept, termed as self-serving bias.

Self-serving bias simply means to blame the outside forces for failures. It's like praising yourself, lifting up your confidence. But in reality, you do it just to be on a safer side. Basically, you do not want to be held responsible for your actions.

For example, Since we are talking about failure let's talk about examinations, if you crack an exam it is because you would say you studied very hard. Similarly, if you fail, you would say the teacher didn't check my paper properly or she anyways didn't teach well.

We all, sometimes, are blaming the outside forces for our failure. It is very common nowadays.

For example, if someone in your office asks, why are you late today? You spontaneously say sir, there was too much traffic today or my bike, car broke down.

If you could lie so easily all the time, just think of how many times you have blamed someone unjustly or judged wrongly? This is proof that next time you hear anybody speaking unjustly about anyone, just separate yourself from them. Get rid of the negativity. "Listen to everyone but be wise enough to do what you want". Choose to be on the brighter side always. Don't let people take advantage of you. Separating yourself from them is not bad. You are doing so because you do not want to end up fighting. It's a very smart move. So just do it. Don't over think or pity yourself.

CHAPTER SIX

REFRAIN FROM JUDGING OTHERS

"Do not speak evil against one another, brothers. The one who speaks against a brother or judges his brother, speaks evil against the law and judges the law. But if you judge the law, you are not a doer of the law but a judge". There is only one lawgiver and judge, he who is able to save and to destroy, but who are you to judge your neighbor? (James 4:11,12). You must have heard people saying, "karma will pay you back". In other words, you give control of your life to God. Exactly the same way, we do not have the right to judge anybody for any reason whatsoever yet, you find people gossiping, speaking evil, making up stories about you. Some people act so stubborn that they don't plan to change even a bit. It's like, hello!! "I'm the boss here".

I would advise you to keep away from such people who are always doing negative things around you. If they do not understand your value, they are certainly not worth having you. Boycott them immediately from your life. Be with those loving, cheerful doing good to others, sharing and bighearted people. The more positive people around, you will think and act like them. If you go around gossiping about people, doing evil and unworthy things, being jealous, rude, holding grudges then, for sure you are roaming around with the wrong bunch of people. Be wise enough to select which category you choose to be with. For example, a verse from the Bible says,

"And whatever town or village you enter, find out who is worthy in it and stay there until you depart". As you enter the house, greet it. And if the house is worthy, let your peace come upon it, but it is not worthy, let your peace return to you.

And if anyone will not receive you or listen to your words, shake off the dust from your feet when you leave that house or town (Matthew 10:11-14).

Jesus always spoke in parables and so are his scriptures in the bible. When Jesus is speaking about town or village, where he is referring to people, friends, telling us how to recognize people who come into your life at any possible stage. He says, find out who is worthy of you. When you make your friend, treat them well. If that particular person(friend) is worthy of you, bless him but, if not worthy which means, if your friend cannot understand you or is speaking wrong about you it could be your family members also. If they are continuously spreading wrong rumors about you. The amount that you blessed them with will come back to you. He also furthermore, explains if they do not listen to you and still continue to do what they always do. He says, to shake off the dust from your feet and leave them. They do not deserve you at all. Just let them go. Probably, not a good match for you. One should have the power to recognize people. It's not possible for us to be friends with everyone. If a person ignores you, don't go behind them. They simply do not deserve you and will probably never appreciate whatever you do.

SILENCE IS THE BEST ANSWER

"Whoever restrains his words has the knowledge, and he who has a cool spirit is a man of understanding. Even a fool who keeps silent is considered wise; when he closes his lips, he is deemed intelligent" (Proverbs 17:27,28).

Sometimes I think being silent is always beneficial? Is keeping quiet the best answer to our enemies? Well, I always felt, it's best to revert back so that they don't keep troubling you again and again. But, honestly not a good idea. Well, you would wonder, what wrong did I do? Even if you would have done nothing yet, you find people talking wrong and rubbish about you anyways. As I said earlier some people will always be there to continuously poke you, make you feel irritated, will oppose you even if they are wrong themselves. Well, don't worry as the lord says, "he who has a cool spirit is a man of understanding". Persecution is definitely coming to my dearest brothers and sisters. For within persecution, there is hidden victory. Silence confuses the enemy because he doesn't know what you're thinking and going to do next. It's frustrating for him. People who persistently annoy or harass you, do not expect them to change because the satan is always at work. Even if you don't call the satan, he is anyways ready to do evil and find a niche to fit himself in. Learn to find a way out instead of giving up on those people. By (satan) I mean the devil which you cannot see with your naked eye. It's in the spiritual realm. The metaphysical world which deals with good and evil spirits. I came across this beautiful quote during my college days and it touched my heart so much that I wanted to know more about it. It says, "The Highest result of education is TOLERANCE". By Hellen Keller.

If you are educated but speak nonsense out of your mouth, people are definitely going to question your education indeed. Most of the time, we tend to just speak out some words and we slowly increase our voice as well as words immediately. Not realizing that you're speaking what you weren't supposed to. Later on, you finally feel that you made a big mistake. So why realize later on and not learn to control your mouth before you speak? Tolerance is an emotion which according to the experience gives you maturity, healthy understanding and makes you mentally strong. This particular emotion will erase your negativity and fill you with complete positive vibes.

For example: If your heart hurts when you let go of someone or something, it is absolutely fine. Because it means that your feelings were genuine. No one likes ends. And no one likes pain. When you lose your dear ones. We feel so depressed and heartbroken. But what do we all do? We learn to tolerate the pain, it doesn't matter how much hurt you are. But you have no option other than to adjust to that pain. Because life is full of compromises, adjustments, sacrifice whenever needed. To tolerate means to be silent and say nothing. Your wisdom comes from being silent.

Learn to Mind Your Own Business

And to aspire to live quietly, and to mind your own business, and to work with your hands, as we instructed you, so that you may walk properly before outsiders and be dependent on no one. 1Thessalonians (4:11,12).

Psychologically speaking, people who feel they are unworthy, insignificant, undeserving. They think they know better, they would basically do anything to show off that they are right. I sometimes think maybe they are tired of themselves, probably bored and disconnected from people. So for their entertainment they try to poke their nose elsewhere. It keeps them busy. Such people are so unhappy about themselves that they tend to hinder about here and there. And they then distract others with their unhappiness. They will impose their beliefs onto you and tell you what would look best on you or rather, will convince you to do it. Whenever you find people who keep interfering into your affairs. Just ignore and get past them immediately. Your intuition will help you know your fake friends, those who give fake smiles, compliment you and insult you at the same time. You will know them by their fruits. According to the scripture in (Matthew 7: 16-20) the lord says, 'You will recognize them by their fruits. And grapes gathered from thornbushes, or figs from thistles. So, every healthy tree cannot bear bad fruit, nor can a diseased tree bear good fruit. A healthy tree cannot bear bad fruit, nor can a diseased tree bear good fruit. Every tree that does not bear good fruit is cut down and thrown into the fire. Thus you will recognize them by their fruits'.

God will give you the power to differentiate between good- bad, right-wrong, good healthy friends - fake diseased friends. As revealed in (Proverbs 20:11) that "Even small children are known by their actions, so is their conduct really pure and upright" ?

Be alert and wise enough to recognize such people. "Let these people who are evildoer still do evil, and the filthy still be filthy, and the righteous still do right, and the holy still be holy"(Revelation 22:11).

But you mind your own business. Focus on your life instead of focusing on others' lives. He says, behold I am coming soon, bringing my recompense with me, to repay each one for what he has done. He will do justice at that time. Then you won't get a second chance, because now is the right time to change. Going to the church every Sunday, sitting and praising god but holding grudges against someone won't let you enter into the kingdom of God. Now is the right time to change, repent, ask for forgiveness. Because later on, god will say, who are you ? I don't know you. And he won't recognise you because we didn't follow his laws to enter into his kingdom(Matthew 7: 21-23).

There is one and only one way to live a more peaceful, tension free and guilt free life and that is to have a pure heart.

Stop holding grudges against people, let go because letting go gives peace to you not them. Forgive so that you may also be forgiven, nobody is perfect and we as humans will keep making mistakes. So, there is no other way but to forgive. To forgive is like an order from god, it's not an option only then comes peace. Dawnn Karen a fashion psychologist, wrote an article on Accepting the Judgment and moved on. She said, " When people worry about judgment, they often make a mistake of believing they can prevent it from happening so I will be judged and what can I do about it"? Whether you change the place or get another job, the other place will too have such kind of people around you. So you need to deal with them not run from them. You will come across some hypocrites who will speak smooth and pleasant words, hiding their wicked heart, be careful because they are deceiving you. They pretend to be kind but are filled with negativity, evil thoughts, planning against you in their hearts. They are backstabbers who want to know everything, not because they care, but so they can gossip. Just imagine how much they talk about you when you're not around. Break that friendship, go away and ignore such people. They simply don't deserve you. Maintain distance with them. Yes, you have to forgive them but at the same time stay away. Learn to deal with such people. Do not run away from the situation. What will you do then? How much are you gonna keep running? Distance yourself from them. Live in peace as well as let them live too. Because trust me when I am saying that life is too short. So live peacefully and protect that peace. A man is blessed abundantly only when he has peace. You may be filthy rich and have everything but if peace is missing. Believe me everything will just break down. So ask God for his ultimate peace. And you will lead a very healthy life.

THANK YOU

www.ingramcontent.com/pod-product-compliance
Lightning Source LLC
Chambersburg PA
CBHW051426250726
48655CB00003B/1264